being a makeup artist

Mary Colson

Lerner Publications Company
Minneapolis

cover stories

24, 28

SHOW ME
Create your own red-carpet looks with the On the Radar makeover guide!

30

REAL-LIFE STORY
Discover what it's like to be a real-life star maker!

18

TOP FIVE
Learn the best makeup tricks in the business.

10

ZONE IN
Find out about other fields where professional makeup artists shine.

First American edition published in 2013 by Lerner Publishing Group, Inc. Published by arrangement with Wayland, a division of Hachette Children's Books

Copyright © 2012 by Wayland

Lerner Publications Company
A division of Lerner Publishing Group, Inc.
241 First Avenue North
Minneapolis, MN U.S.A.

Website address: www.lernerbooks.com

Library of Congress
Cataloging-in-Publication Data

Colson, Mary.
    Being a makeup artist / by Mary Colson.
      p.   cm. — (On the radar: awesome jobs)
    Includes index.
    ISBN 978-0-7613-7777-1 (lib. bdg. : alk. paper)
    1. Theatrical makeup—Juvenile literature. 2. Film makeup—Juvenile literature. 3. Television makeup—Juvenile literature. 4. Performing arts—Vocational guidance—Juvenile literature. I. Title.
PN2068.C585 2013
792.02'7023—dc23   2011052672

Manufactured in the United States of America
– CG – 7/15/12

Acknowledgments: Myriam Djellouli: 2c, 31; Julian Watson Agency: 22, 22–23; Cassie Lomas: cover, 16l, 16–17, 17r; Mitsuki McCormack: 10b, 15b; Rex: FoxSearch/Everett 20; Shutterstock: Subbotina Anna 12–13, cinemafestival 1, 19br, Olga Ekaterincheva 7, Helga Esteb 9, 15tl, 15tc, 19tr, 26, Raisa Kanareva 11br, krivenko 3br, Luba V Nel 10t, PhotoStock10 1l, Joe Seer 3bl, 4–5, 18–19, Gina Smith 2b, 11tr, stocklight 24tl, 28t, Valua Vitaly 8, Carla Van Wagoner 12–13, Vladimir Wrangel 6.

Main body text set in
Helvetica Neue LT Std 13/15.5.
Typeface provided by Adobe Systems.

thepeople

theart

thetalk

Glamorous stars tread Hollywood's red carpet, actors light up the big screen, and celebrities fill the glossy pages of magazines. But who is behind their flawless looks?

A-LIST LOOKS

Lights, camera—sparkle!

Celebrity makeup artists are responsible for improving and maximizing stars' looks so that they shine in the spotlight.

Makeup artists help actors create the look of their characters. The artists also make up other famous people, including celebrities and politicians. Makeup artists ensure their clients can be photographed with hundreds of flashing bulbs while still looking great.

The jet set

Makeup artists work on film and TV sets, in theater productions, and at the world's fashion shows. In countless locations, from Paris, France, and London, England, to New York and Tokyo, Japan. A-list celebrities—such as Nicole Scherzinger *(right)*—know the value of a top makeup artist. Many even fly their favorite artist to wherever they are in the world to create a look for a photo shoot or an important appearance, such as a film premiere.

Making it

To be a great makeup artist, you don't need to be good at art or able to draw, but you do need a strong sense of color, style, and imagination. On top of that, you need a lot of practice; a bit of luck; and if you want to make it to the top, a real passion for the job.

Macho makeup

Makeup artists work on male celebrities too. Stars such as Ben Stiller, Johnny Depp, and Robert Pattinson have their faces worked on before they go on a film set, appear on TV, or make an entrance at an awards ceremony.

CENTURIES OF COSMETICS

For centuries, people have experimented with makeup and created dramatic looks using whatever ingredients they could find.

The famous bust of Nefertiti, the wife of the Egyptian pharaoh Akhenaton, shows her with heavily kohled eyes.

Strictly no tanning

In the Middle Ages (from A.D. 500–1500), wealthy women covered their faces with lead paint or powder. They wore pink lipstick to show they could afford to buy cosmetics. Prostitutes, on the other hand, painted their faces pink to distinguish themselves in a crowd.

All made up

The ancient Egyptians were all about Cleopatra eyes! They used luminous green eye shadow made from copper powder and heavy black lines made from a mixture of soot and kohl (black powder). Later, the Romans used chalk to whiten their faces and henna (a reddish dye) to color their hair. They also used beetroot juice to create lipstick and blusher.

Colonial cover-up

Smallpox was a disease that often left survivors with pockmarks (small pits) on their skin. Colonial Americans—both male and female—used makeup to cover their blemishes. They made white face powder from readily available foodstuffs, such as flour and cornstarch.

Victorian cheek

In the 1800s, wearing makeup was thought to be vulgar. But many women used makeup to enhance their complexion. They crushed flower petals, for example, to add a tinge of pink to their cheeks or lips. Soot acted as a cheap and available way to bring drama to the eyes. Britain's stuffy Queen Victoria highly disapproved.

Max Factor to wow factor

The makeup created by Russian immigrant Max Factor was used in early Hollywood films to create a dramatic look for stars such as Rudolph Valentino. Davis Factor, the grandson of the makeup pioneer, has invented his own brand, Smashbox, which creates cosmetics that aim to provide a flawless finish on camera for modern stars.

Modern makeup artists and the models they work with are credited with setting new makeup trends that are followed by people around the world.

BEAUTY BANTER

Give your vocab a makeover with the ultimate On the Radar guide!

bronzer
a powder or cream applied to the skin to give it a sun-kissed glow

concealer
a cream or powder that covers up pimples, scars, and eye bags

palette
a collection of matching shades of eye shadow, lipstick, or blusher

call time
the time you need to be on set or in the studio, ready to work

foundation
powder or liquid that is applied before any makeup to give skin an even color and to cover any blemishes

portfolio
a paper or digital folder with photos of a makeup artist's previous work

character sheet
used on film and TV sets, this has all the key information about a character's look and personality

kohl
a black powder used as eye makeup

shadow stick
a smooth eye shadow used to create smoky eyes

matte
natural-looking makeup that is not glossy

tear stick
a special wax that has tear-making chemicals

False eyelashes and rich colors are used to create dramatic eyes.

toner
a liquid that is applied to the skin to remove cleanser and tighten skin pores. It is also part of a cleansing routine before and after makeup.

undertone
the natural colors that lie beneath your skin. Makeup artists base their color choices on a client's undertones.

touch-ups
final adjustments to makeup before the cameras roll

GLOSSARY

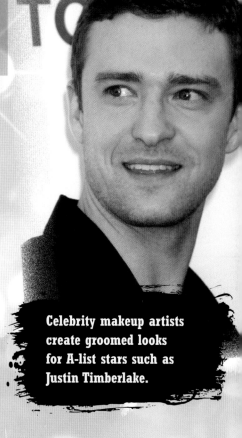

Celebrity makeup artists create groomed looks for A-list stars such as Justin Timberlake.

A-list
the most famous people in the entertainment and film industry

arsenic
a deadly poison

BAFTA
the British Academy of Film and Television Arts

end roll credits/ film credits
the list of actors and other professionals in a film, shown at the end of the film

fine arts
a college course that focuses on how to create art as well as the history of art

flawless
perfect and unmarked in any way

freelance
when someone is self-employed and works for different companies on short-term contracts

henna
a reddish dye made from the powdered leaves of a plant

iconic
instantly recognizable and influential

latex
a type of rubber

lead
a soft, poisonous metal that is blue gray in color

premiere
the first viewing of a film

timeless
something that does not date

vulgar
tasteless; indecent

wrap
the end of filming

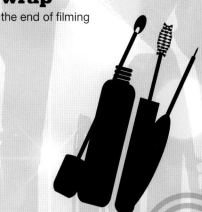

THE LOOKS

Makeup is much more than a touch of lipstick or a dab of powder. From celebrity glamour and catwalk cool to award-winning film and TV faces, makeup artists work in many different fields to create the outrageous, the extravagant, and the extraordinary.

Camera and catwalk

Catwalk and photographic makeup is more dramatic and thickly applied than the makeup looks created for TV, film, or an awards ceremony. For the launch of MAC's 2011 range, the makeup giant turned its back on traditional looks. It hired revolutionary makeup artist Cindy Sherman to design new looks. Cindy made up models' faces to look like clowns, with white faces; exaggerated eyebrows; and huge, brightly colored lips.

Looking the part

Stage, or cake, makeup has to be seen from a distance and under bright lights, so it is thickly applied or caked on. Theatrical makeup helps to create different characters, from white-faced, red-lipped dames to dark-eyed tragic heroes.

Changing bodies

Artificial latex shapes are used to change appearances such as the shape of a nose. Larger fake pieces can create weird and wonderful aliens and monsters.

Call 9-1-1!

Fake blood powder, plastic bone bits, stick-on scars, and sweat drops are in every film set makeup kit. Using these products, makeup artists can re-create everything from accidents and operations to murder scenes. Some of the most inventive makeup work takes place on thriller or horror film sets.

Photographic makeup is thickly applied to ensure it looks good under a camera lens.

fake zits!

Catwalk makeup *(above and top right)* is often highly dramatic and designed to help create a story that complements the designer's clothing range.

Stage makeup helps to create a character and is heavily applied so that it is visible from a distance.

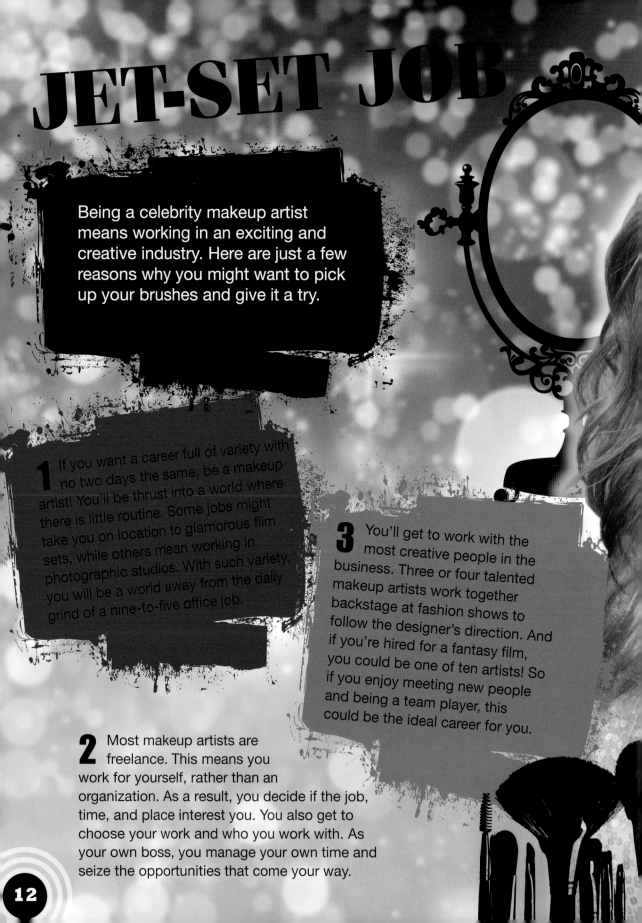

JET-SET JOB

Being a celebrity makeup artist means working in an exciting and creative industry. Here are just a few reasons why you might want to pick up your brushes and give it a try.

1 If you want a career full of variety with no two days the same, be a makeup artist! You'll be thrust into a world where there is little routine. Some jobs might take you on location to glamorous film sets, while others mean working in photographic studios. With such variety, you will be a world away from the daily grind of a nine-to-five office job.

3 You'll get to work with the most creative people in the business. Three or four talented makeup artists work together backstage at fashion shows to follow the designer's direction. And if you're hired for a fantasy film, you could be one of ten artists! So if you enjoy meeting new people and being a team player, this could be the ideal career for you.

2 Most makeup artists are freelance. This means you work for yourself, rather than an organization. As a result, you decide if the job, time, and place interest you. You also get to choose your work and who you work with. As your own boss, you manage your own time and seize the opportunities that come your way.

4 The most talented makeup artists are invited to film screenings and post-premiere parties. You could socialize with the stars, such as Hayden Panettiere *(left)*, whose makeup you have created. Just like them, your name will be on the film's credits. If the makeup is central to the look of the film, you could even make a name for yourself as a star and then it could be *you* onstage accepting an award!

MITSUKI McCORMACK

On the Radar consultant Mitsuki McCormack has been a makeup artist to film stars and celebrities for 10 years. We interviewed Mitsuki to find out all about her glamorous job.

What inspired you to become a makeup artist?

I was studying art and fashion but wasn't quite sure which career path was best for me. A friend introduced me to a makeup artist, and I helped him at a fashion photo shoot. Right away, I knew it was the job for me.

What's been your career highlight so far?

Working for celebrities is fun, but being asked to create corpses for the film *Moon in Gemini* has taken my career into a great new area. Making people look hideous is just as much fun as making them look fabulous!

What is the best thing about your job?

I'm able to design new looks, work with artistic people, be as creative as I like. Seeing my name in the credits really is the icing on the cake!

And the worst?

I would say it's probably the long working hours. On average, I work 10-hour days, if not more (and often with no lunch break!), when I'm working on a film or TV set.

Which stars would you like to create a look for?

Top of the list are stars with expressive faces, such as Christina Ricci (*above left*) and Mila Kunis (*above right*), who are both beautiful and open-minded about creating different looks.

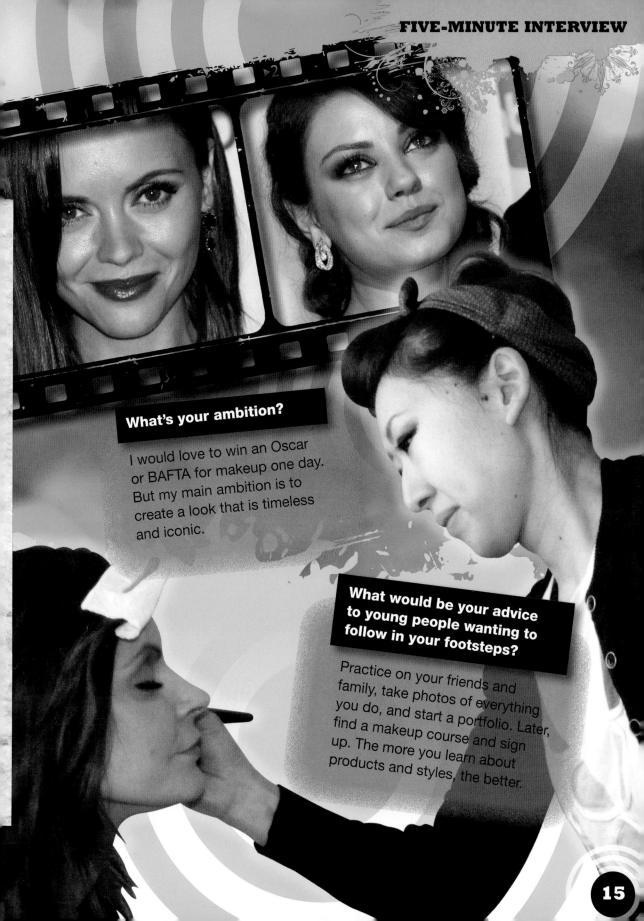

What's your ambition?

I would love to win an Oscar or BAFTA for makeup one day. But my main ambition is to create a look that is timeless and iconic.

What would be your advice to young people wanting to follow in your footsteps?

Practice on your friends and family, take photos of everything you do, and start a portfolio. Later, find a makeup course and sign up. The more you learn about products and styles, the better.

A week in the life of a celebrity makeup artist

CASSIE LOMAS

blog   news   events

Monday

There has been no routine whatsoever to my life as a makeup artist! Last year, I toured with Lady Gaga for six months. Being away from home was hard. This year I am focusing on teaching students at my makeup academy. I started the academy from scratch, so it has taken all my energy to make it a success.

Tuesday

I left home at 7 A.M. to work on a talk show. I got to the studios at 12 P.M. and did hair and makeup for two hours. We wrapped at 4 P.M., after the show had been filmed.

blog | news | events

Wednesday

At 8 A.M., I left home to work on the set for a new TV show. I was a guest on the show as the makeup artist creating new looks for women. We wrapped at 7 P.M., but I didn't get home until midnight—I fell straight into bed, I was so tired!

Thursday

Photo shoot today at the academy. This meant the students were presenting their makeup designs on real models for the first time. There were students, models, and makeup kits everywhere! It was a real buzz!

Friday

I spent the day filming more episodes of the new show. Call time on the show was 7 A.M., so I was up before 6 A.M. to get myself ready. We wrapped at 3 P.M.

Saturday

I taught a basic beauty course at the academy all day. You have to be dedicated in this business. My work has always come first, so I've never had a lot of time off!

Sunday

I managed to have some downtime and a family dinner today—a rare treat! I don't mind though. My job is amazing, and I wouldn't want to do anything else.

TOOL BAG TIPS

True celebrity makeup artists will do anything to achieve the perfect looks for their clients. Here are the professional makeup artists' best tricks of the trade.

1. Perfect base

All makeup artists insist on working with perfectly cleansed and smooth skin. If an artist has no gloss on hand, sugar is fantastic at removing dead skin. The makeup artist pours a little white sugar into the palm of the hand, mixes in a few drops of water, and then rubs the homemade exfoliator onto the skin. Rough skin is removed, and the complexion is given an instant pink glow, just the way Katie Holmes *(right)* likes it.

2. Top brushes

A great makeup artist invests in top-quality makeup brushes. Many makeup artists buy some of their brushes from artist supply shops because of the excellent quality of their brush fibers.

3. Gorgeous lips

Before applying lipstick or lip gloss, makeup artists prepare the lips by rubbing them with a toothbrush dipped in a little water and sugar. This removes any flaky skin and plumps up the lips so that any lipstick they apply does not crease or crack. Victoria Justice *(right)* shows how the trick works.

4. Sparkling eyes

Makeup artists never go anywhere without tea bags! When wet, they make fantastic eye pads and help to restore A-list sparkle to tired eyes. If put in the fridge for five minutes before use, tea bags also cool and freshen sore eyes.

5. Tub of magic

Many makeup artists swear by Vaseline. It has a multitude of uses. It can be used to soothe dry and chapped skin and is ideal for holding groomed eyebrows in place. Last, but not least, it can be used as gloss over lipstick to create a luscious, perfect pout, like the one sported by Scarlett Johansson *(right)*.

JUDY CHIN

Makeup's leading lady

When Judy designed the looks for Natalie Portman *(right)* in *Black Swan* (2010), she used dramatic makeup to convey the dark side of Portman's character.

Painting with makeup

Judy studied fine arts and film at college, and in 1988, she moved to New York City. She took a job at the New York City Opera, where she spent four years creating looks for the dancers and developing her stage makeup skills. Judy soon discovered that she could use makeup to create a sense of the dancer's stage character.

An artist at work

Judy's screen career began in the early 1990s, when she worked on the TV show *Monsters*. Judy believed that makeup could create an emotion or a feeling as well as an image. She drew portraits of the characters she made up to establish their personality and mood. She soon became famous for the great attention she gave to the fine details that could convey aspects of a character's personality.

Into film

Judy's artistry was soon in demand in the film world. Her talent was showcased in productions such as *The Tempest* (2010). Judy also became the personal makeup artist to actress Sarah Jessica Parker on many films, including *Did You Hear about the Morgans?* (2009).

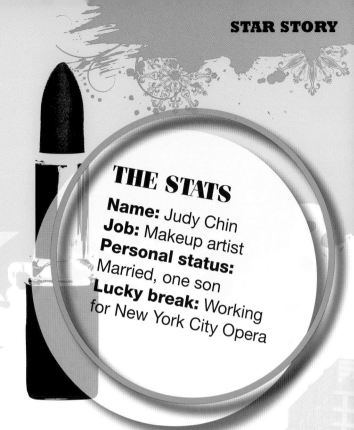

THE STATS

Name: Judy Chin
Job: Makeup artist
Personal status: Married, one son
Lucky break: Working for New York City Opera

Film star's favorite

Judy is constantly in demand with directors and actors alike. Her sense of design and her understanding of character are what make stars such as Parker, Ben Stiller, Jennifer Connelly, and Rachel Weisz ask for her time after time.

Career highlights

2000–2010 personal makeup artist to Jennifer Connelly, Rachel Weisz, and Sarah Jessica Parker for various films

2002 won an Oscar for her work on *Frida*, a film about the artist Frida Kahlo

2011 nominated for a BAFTA (British movie award) for *Black Swan*

2013 personal makeup artist to Weisz on *Oz: The Great and the Powerful*

HANNAH MURRAY

Early dreams

As a young girl, Hannah dreamed of being a ballerina. With years of training, she made her dream come true and became a professional dancer. Then, suddenly, she was forced to rethink her whole future when she injured her ankle. After three ankle operations, Hannah realized she would never dance again. Luckily, she had more than one talent. Hannah had always loved makeup and had made up the other dancers before shows. She decided that this could be her new career.

THE STATS

Name: Hannah Murray
Born: January 30, 1979
Nationality: British
Based in: London, England

Makeup superstar

In 2010 Hannah was invited to become the makeup consultant for Topshop, which has stores in London, New York, and Chicago. She has helped to create new makeup ranges inspired by themes such as the Amazon, sandstorms, and heavy metal. These days Hannah travels the world, works with the best in the business, and has made her mark as a talented makeup artist. In constant demand by fashion houses, magazines, and superstars, Hannah is one of the hottest global artists.

Big break

In 1998, at 19 years of age, Hannah took an eight-week course at the famous Glauca Rossi School of Makeup in London. Her big break was when she became first assistant to Charlotte Tilbury, one of the world's leading makeup artists. Hannah spent two years with Charlotte, working with her every day and traveling the world while she learned about the business.

Cover girl

After her demanding schedule with Charlotte, Hannah had learned enough to launch her own career. In 2008 she made up Victoria Beckham for the star's first cover shoot for British *Vogue*. Since then, Hannah has styled dozens of covers for magazines and has worked with some of the world's top photographers, including Mario Testino. She's made up celebrities such as Alexa Chung and Lady Gaga.

AMAZING EYES!

Follow the step-by-step guide to smoky eyes to re-create Rihanna's *(left)* look!

You will need:

- **pale gray eye shadow**
- **dark gray eye shadow**
- **2 eye shadow brushes**
- **black eye pencil and mascara**

1 Use a pale gray eye shadow to cover the whole of the eyelid from lash line to eyebrow.

2 Dip another brush into the dark gray eye shadow. Use it to shade along the lash line.

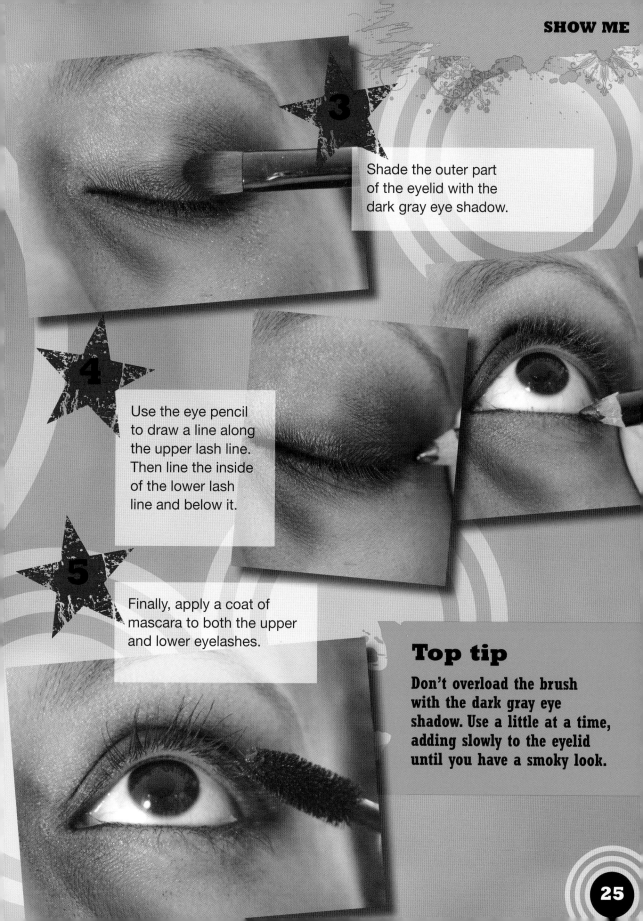

3

Shade the outer part of the eyelid with the dark gray eye shadow.

4

Use the eye pencil to draw a line along the upper lash line. Then line the inside of the lower lash line and below it.

5

Finally, apply a coat of mascara to both the upper and lower eyelashes.

Top tip

Don't overload the brush with the dark gray eye shadow. Use a little at a time, adding slowly to the eyelid until you have a smoky look.

MAKING A DIFFERENCE

Not content to stay behind the scenes in the dressing room, a few celebrity makeup artists are using cosmetics to make a difference.

Eco-aware

Getting a great look that is also environmentally friendly is fast becoming the style of many makeup artists. With increased awareness of natural products and organic ingredients, many artists are turning their backs on the chemical-filled creams and applications of the past.

Celebrity makeup artist Lina Hanson is one of a growing number of artists who use only ecofriendly products. Her eco-aware A-list clients include Naomi Watts, Mandy Moore, and Zac Efron (left).

Made with minerals

One of the most recent trends in modern makeup is the use of minerals to create pure, chemical-free makeup that does not block skin pores. The company Bare Escentuals started the concept with its range of mineral-based powders, Bare Minerals. The brand describes the range as "makeup so pure you can sleep in it" and has a celebrity fan base including Jennifer Aniston and Natalie Portman. The brand proved so popular that other

Many celebrities are fans of organic cosmetics and skin-friendly mineral makeup (above).

cosmetic giants, such as L'Oréal and MAC, have since launched their own mineral-based makeup ranges.

Life beyond lipstick

Bobbi Brown is a hugely successful U.S. makeup consultant and author, who tries to make a difference with her charity work. Through Dress for Success, Bobbi provides underprivileged women with clothes and makeovers to help give them the confidence to attend job interviews.

Whether it's improving people's lives or protecting the planet, the cosmetics industry is showing that makeup really can make a difference.

LOVELY LIPS!

Here's how to re-create Rihanna's perfect peachy pout!

You will need:

- peachy-colored lip liner
- lipstick
- lip gloss
- lipstick brush

1 Begin by lining the lips with a peachy-colored lip liner.

2 Use the lipstick brush to apply lipstick to the lips.

3 Apply lip gloss. This will add a sheer, shimmery finish to the lipstick.

Top tip

Using a brush to apply the lipstick will ensure that you get a perfectly smooth finish. Complete the look by applying a peachy-toned blusher to your cheekbones.

STAR MAKER

My story by Mimi D

Ever since I was a little girl, I have been fascinated by makeup. One day, my aunt gave me her favorite pink lipstick, and I decided there and then to turn my passion into a career and become a makeup artist.

I read everything I could about makeup. I tore out interesting articles on different types of makeup from magazines and kept them in a file. I still add ideas to my file even now.

I spent hours practicing on friends and clients and kept a photographic record of the looks I created to build up my portfolio. I also worked for free to gain experience and contacts. I worked in makeup studios, in fashion shops, and at makeup counters, which was a great way to learn. I did a theatrical and media makeup course and then became the national trainer for a major French cosmetic company.

Now I work as a freelance makeup artist. One day I'll be doing a photo shoot for an advertising campaign, the next day, a private client's wedding. The following day, I might do a glamorous fashion show, and then the next day, I might be making up a celebrity client. I can't leave the house without a suitcase and a travel bag. I take about 50 eye shadows with me and then about 20 of every other product!

The best thing about my job is that it never feels like a job. I'm my own boss, I have my own website, I work with artistic people, and I get to be creative every day. One day, I'd love to do Madonna's makeup—so, if you see her, remember to give her my number!

GET MORE INFO

Books

Academy of Freelance Makeup. *Makeup Is Art: Professional Techniques for Creating Original Looks*. London: Carlton Books, 2011. Makeup artists from London's Academy of Freelance Makeup share advice, instructions, and photos to help create great makeup looks.

Barnes, Scott. *About Face: Amazing Transformations Using the Secrets of the Top Celebrity Makeup Artist.* Minneapolis: Fair Winds Press, 2010. Discover the makeup secrets the author has used on people, from everyday women to A-list celebrities

Brown, Bobbi. *Bobbi Brown Makeup Manual: For Everyone from Beginner to Pro.* New York: Grand Central Life & Style, 2008. Learn all about makeup, skin care, and body care in this book from a leading industry professional.

Sutherland, Adam. *Being a Model.* Minneapolis: Lerner Publications Company, 2013. Find out what it takes to be a model in this On the Radar title.

Thomas, Isabel. *Being a Photographer.* Minneapolis: Lerner Publications Company, 2013. Go behind the camera to see what photographers see through the lens.

Websites

Carmindy
http://www.carmindy.com/
Head to this website for everyday makeup tips from Carmindy, who is on TLC's *What Not to Wear* and appears in top magazines.

Makeup Artist
http://www.makeupmag.com/
Catch up on industry news and hear from Hollywood professionals about their projects on this magazine's website.

INDEX